S is for STILLWATER

S

is for
STILLWATER

This is an A to Z picture book with 26 beautiful illustrations of Stillwater, Minnesota. Each illustration is a watercolor that depicts the history of Stillwater, from past to present. This book includes exciting places for a child to visit, such as Aamodt's Apple Farm and Candyland. It also includes historical buildings and landmarks that are special to Stillwater.

To my parents, who always supported my aspirations.

Ingram Content Group
One Ingram Blvd., La Vergne, TN 37086

Located west of downtown, **Aamodt's Apple** Farm provides apple treats to the public. It definitely is an **autumn** thrill. Right down to the core!

B

Stillwater decorates itself with two historical **bridges**. The **Stone Arch Bridge**, built in 1863, is the oldest known stone arch bridge in Minnesota. Currently adorning the Brown's Creek bike trail, it was built originally to carry the territory's military troops over the creek. In 1876, the first Stillwater Bridge between Minnesota and Wisconsin was built; later rebuilt in 1931 as the **Lift Bridge,** and recently closed to automobile traffic for the last time in 2017. It is one of two lift-style bridges left in the state.

Stillwater also became known as the "**Birthplace** of Minnesota", incorporated as a city in 1854, when a group of concerned citizens organized a convention in order to form a new territory named "Minnesota".

C The Washington County **Courthouse** was built in 1870 on the beautiful "Zion's Hill" location near Pine and 3rd Streets. This building has an attractive copper dome, and is a popular wedding location.

The Freight **Depot**, is listed on the National Register of Historic Places. Built in 1883, the structure originally serviced train passengers and freight to the cities of St. Paul, Milwaukee, and Chicago. Currently a restaurant, it expands along the St. Croix riverfront.

E

Education was and still is important to Stillwater residents. In 1902, the Stillwater Public Library opened. The money for the ornamental building was donated by Andrew Carnegie, a wealthy railroad owner.

One of Minnesota's first public schoolhouses was built in Stillwater in 1848. Boutwell School District 2, became one of the first school districts in Minnesota a few years later.

Festivals, fireworks and fairs! Stillwater brings the community together year-round with a number of festivals. Lumberjack Days, held each summer, celebrates the logging industry with a festival.

During the middle of a beautiful, autumn weekend, Lowell Park in Stillwater provides entertainment, arts, and good food to celebrate the fall season. A Harvest Festival highlight is the pumpkin drop from a crane high in the air. Some of the festival's largest pumpkins weighing nearly 2,000 pounds are world records!

Other festivals include the 4th of July fireworks, art fairs, and most recently, the Ice Castles during winter.

G

On a warm summer evening, you may see a long, black **gondola** with a man standing at the end. The "**gondolier**" steers with a long oar on the flat-bottomed row boat.

The Commander building, originally a **grain elevator,** was built in the last part of the 1800s and held grain for the flour mills nearby. Currently, it serves as a cafe with the fitting name, "Tin Bins".

Rising up over the treetops of Aamodt's Apple Farm, you can see sudden bursts of color in the sky. Not one, but two or three brightly colored **hot air balloons** take an early evening glide above the river valley.

I scream, you scream, we all scream for **ice cream!** A great summer treat after baseball or soccer means going to one of the many local ice cream shops!

J

The **Jail,** or in other words, the Minnesota Territorial Prison, housed prisoners from around the region years ago. Some members of Jesse James' gang were imprisoned there! In 1856, there was a mass escape by every prisoner. Sadly, after the prison was moved down the road into Oak Park Heights, the vacant prison was destroyed by fire in 2002. However, the Warden's House currently exists next door.

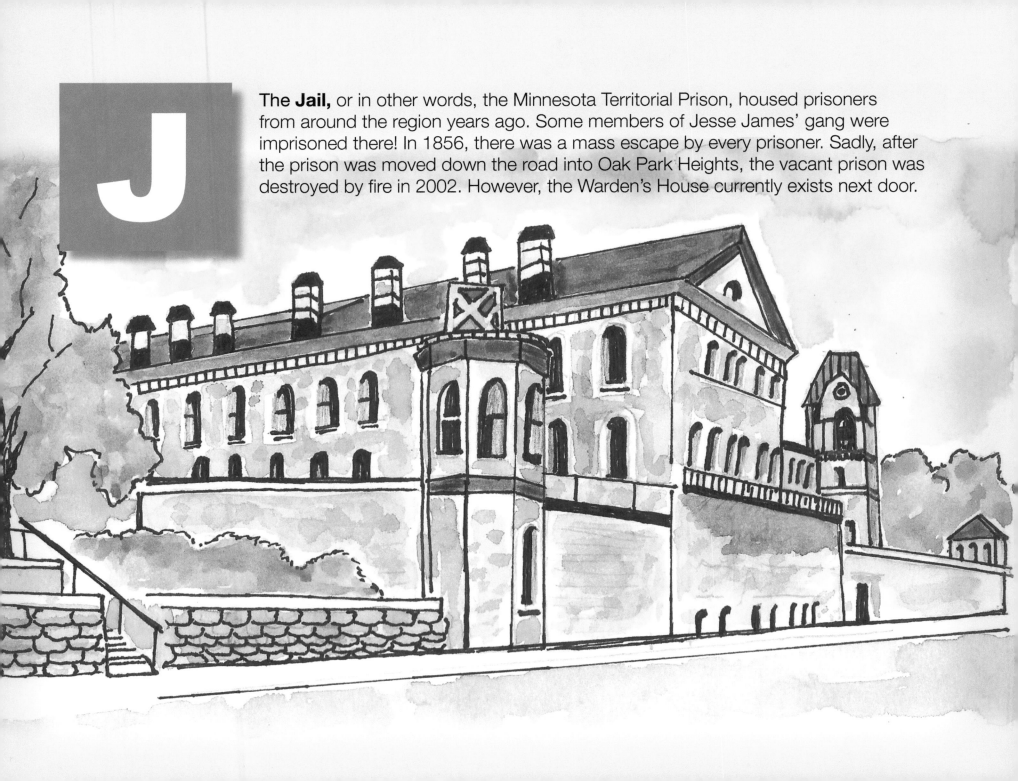

Kiddos galore! Teddy Bear Park is the perfect setting for busy fun! Younger kids can keep climbing on swings and ropes, while older children climb the rock wall that is naturally formed from the nearby cave.

Logging made Stillwater a thriving city with mills running along the St. Croix River. Loggers or "boom rats", used a boom, which is a barrier of logs chained together to catch the large logs as they floated downstream. Sometimes, the large logs would pile up into amazing log jams. The current Boom Site, located north of town, was the destination for the logs, collected for the mills to make into lumber.

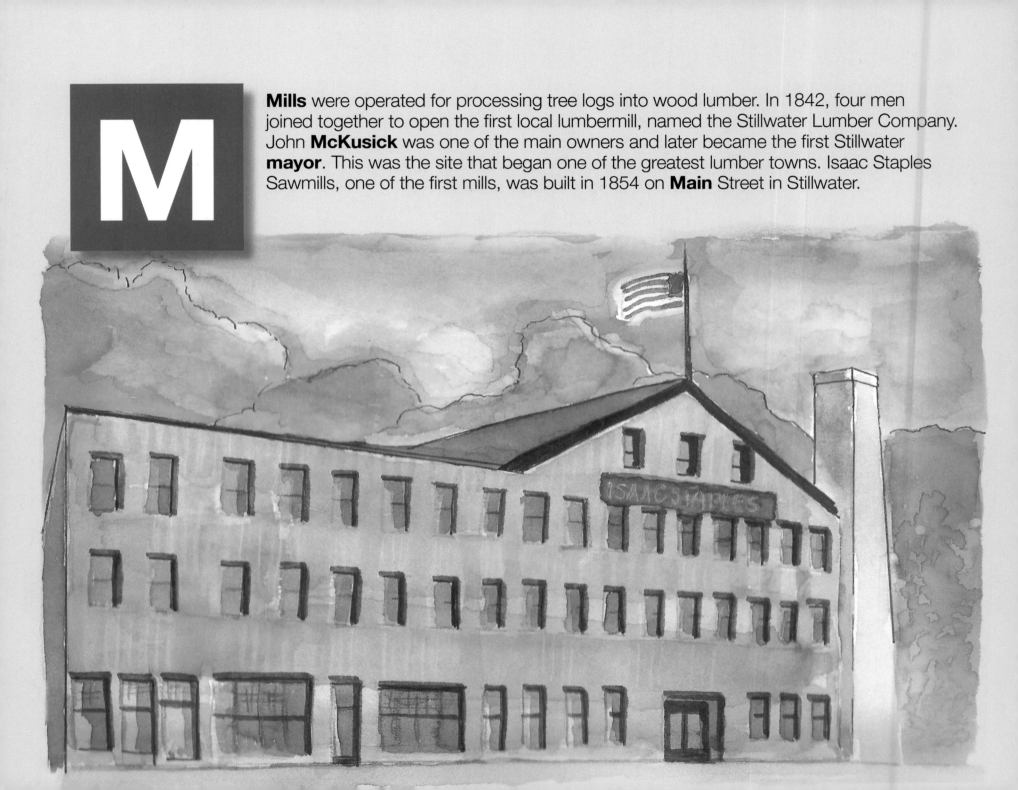

M

Mills were operated for processing tree logs into wood lumber. In 1842, four men joined together to open the first local lumbermill, named the Stillwater Lumber Company. John **McKusick** was one of the main owners and later became the first Stillwater **mayor**. This was the site that began one of the greatest lumber towns. Isaac Staples Sawmills, one of the first mills, was built in 1854 on **Main** Street in Stillwater.

The "**New** Bridge" is formally named the St. Croix River Crossing. This beautifully designed cable bridge, opened in 2017, has 5 pairs of piers. It stands 10 stories above the river. This unusual design makes it only second of its kind in the United States!

In 1837, treaties were signed between the U.S. government and the local **Ojibwe** and Dakota nations that allowed settlement in the St. Croix Valley. The site for the legend of the famous Battle Hollow, near a ravine between the St. Croix Ojibwe and the Dakota groups in 1839, later became the location of the Minnesota Territorial Prison.

The **Pony** is Stillwater Area High School's team mascot. Ponies wearing red and black can proudly be seen all over town. Stillwater Area Public Schools has a reputation of excellence in academics, arts, and athletics. Today, the Stillwater Area School District services over 8,400 students.

Quotes about the
Stillwater Lift Bridge:

The Lift Bridge symbolizes the move of not only
Stillwater but the St. Croix Valley into modern age.
- Washington County Historian Brent Peterson

It separated Stillwater from the lumber era to more of a
manufacturing era, from the horse and buggy to auto mobiles.
- Star Tribune newspaper

The St. Croix **River** is a French word meaning "holy cross", since it expands 169 miles, leading as a tributary into the Mississippi River. Steep, rocky bluffs line the walls of part of the river north of the town.

Riverboats, called paddleboats powered by large wheels or paddles, would carry passengers and cargo down and up the river. Nowadays, we will see other smaller boats exploring the river too.

It has been rumored that if you stand in the right place, you can count **seven steeples** within your view! Stillwater has many churches, each uniquely designed; some with melodic chimes during the course of the day.

T

Also known as street cars, the **trolleys** were a mode of transportation around Stillwater from the early 1900s. Today, the trolley is a tour bus, buzzing around Stillwater without rails.

U

Upstairs

Count how many steps you can climb from the downtown area to see a stunning view of the Lift Bridge! This historic stairway was built to help lead residents from downtown to their homes overlooking the main district. The steps were built alongside the Joseph Wolf caves. Today, many health enthusiasts run or walk the steps for a good workout of about 100 steps!

THIS WAY UP

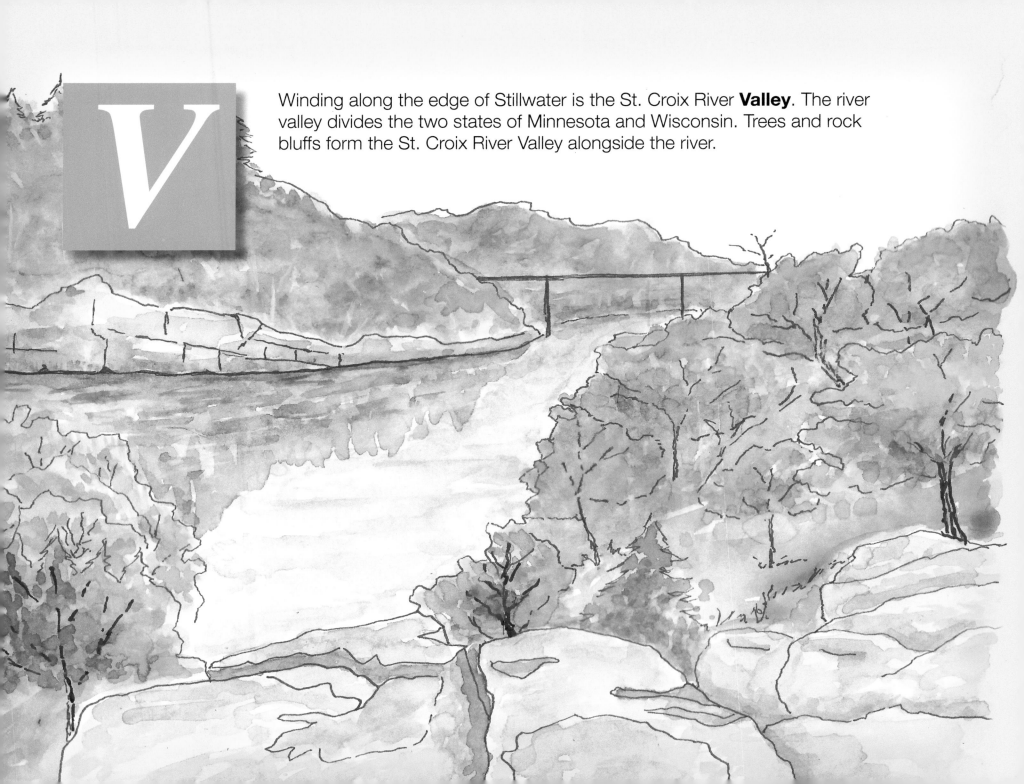

V

Winding along the edge of Stillwater is the St. Croix River **Valley**. The river valley divides the two states of Minnesota and Wisconsin. Trees and rock bluffs form the St. Croix River Valley alongside the river.

Minnesota's main connection with our next door neighbor, **Wisconsin,** comes by means of the St. Croix River. The Lift Bridge between Minnesota and Wisconsin divides Stillwater and Houlton, WI. The new St. Croix River Crossing (New Bridge) is just south of Stillwater. The border battle gets pretty exciting during the football season between the Vikings and the Packers!

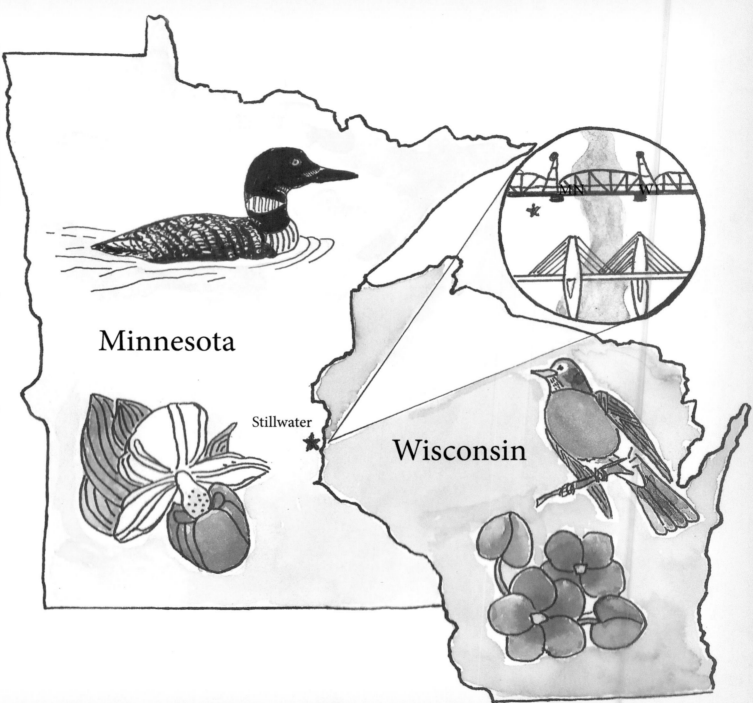

Minnesota

Stillwater

Wisconsin

X

EXtra EXtra, Read All About It! Newspapers have been an important part of Stillwater's history. The *St. Croix Union* in 1854 was a weekly newspaper and the second newspaper, *Stillwater Messenger*, created issues from 1856-1950. The *Stillwater Gazette* was established in 1870, and continues production today. Other newspapers have dissolved, including the languages of *German Der Herman Sohns* and *Scandinavian Vesterlandet*.

Yum–Yum! Stillwater attracts the best candy shops around! There are several on Main Street, including Candyland's delicious carameled popcorn, Tremblay's chocolates, and Barbara Ann's fudge.

Z

For many years, the railroad was a dream for shipping wood out of Stillwater. The rail train finally reached the valley, and as a result shipping was made easier.

The **Zephyr** was a passenger train operating out of Stillwater for many years. The locomotive would travel south along the St. Croix River bluffs, using the first track built in the 1870s. It was a thrill ride for both young and old!

B

Lea Brynestad is a resident of Stillwater and has raised 3 sons with her husband, who helped with the book design.

She is also an elementary art teacher within the Stillwater Area Public Schools.

During her spare time, she enjoys biking down the Brown's Creek trail into Stillwater, and across the new bridge.

CPSIA information can be obtained
at www.ICGtesting.com
Printed in the USA
BVHW092329061019
560381BV00002BA/2/P